THE PUERTO RICANS IN AMERICA

The IN AMERICA *Series*

THE **PUERTO RICANS** IN AMERICA

RONALD J. LARSEN

Published by
Lerner Publications Company
Minneapolis, Minnesota

ACKNOWLEDGMENTS

The illustrations are reproduced through the courtesy of: pp. 6, 9, 10, 11, 13, 14, 17, 19, 23, 34, 42, 47, 50, 72, Independent Picture Service; pp. 12, 21, Institute of Culture, Puerto Rico; p. 15, Puerto Rico Department of Tourism; p. 25 (left and right), National Archives; pp. 26, 32, 35, 43, The Commonwealth of Puerto Rico; pp. 28, 63, Religious News Service; p. 29, Partido Popular Democratico; pp. 30, 31, Puerto Rico Urban Renewal and Housing Corporation; p. 37, *El Mundo*; pp. 39, 48, 75, 77 (top left), 81 (left and right), Wide World Photos; p. 46, The New York Convention and Visitors Bureau, photo by Allen Green; pp. 52, 83, Kenneth G. Lawrence's Movie Memorabilia Shop of Hollywood; pp. 55, 56, 57, 66, United Press International; pp. 59, 65, National Puerto Rican Forum, Incorporated; p. 60, The Puerto Rican Community Development Project, Incorporated; p. 62 (top left), New York Assemblyman Armando Montano; p. 62 (top right), Assembly Chamber, Albany, New York; p. 62 (bottom), The City of New York, Office of the Mayor; p. 64, Martin L. Schneider/Associates; p. 67, ACTION; p. 69, Office of the State Senator, New York; p. 70, Senator Herman Badillo; p. 73, Nick Lugo; p. 74, The Puerto Rican Traveling Theatre Company, Incorporated; p. 76, Piri Thomas; p. 77 (top right and bottom), Festival Casals; pp. 78 (left), 79 (top), George Brace; p. 78 (right), Luis Rodriguez Olmo; p. 79 (bottom left), Three Rivers Stadium, Pittsburgh, Pennsylvania; p. 79 (bottom right), Oakland Stadium, Oakland, California; p. 80 (left and right), The Ring, Incorporated; p. 81 (middle), *World Tennis*; p. 82, RCA Records; p. 84, James Fry, photographer.

LIBRARY OF CONGRESS CATALOGING IN PUBLICATION DATA

Larsen, Ronald J.
  The Puerto Ricans in America.

  (The In America Series)
  SUMMARY: A brief history of Puerto Rico, Puerto Rican immigration to the mainland, and the individual contributions of Puerto Ricans to American life and culture.

  1. Puerto Ricans in the United States—Juvenile literature.
  [1. Puerto Ricans in the United States] I. Title.

  E184.P85L37   301.45'19'687295073   72-3590
  ISBN 0-8225-0225-9

International Standard Book Number: 0-8225-0225-9
Library of Congress Catalog Card Number: 72-3590

...CONTENTS...

Puerto Rico—The Crossroads of the Caribbean

The great chain of islands lying between North and South America and separating the Atlantic Ocean from the Caribbean Sea is known as the West Indies. This island chain is divided into three parts: the Bahamas, the Greater Antilles, and the Lesser Antilles. The most important of these groups is the Greater Antilles, which includes the islands of Cuba, Jamaica, Hispaniola (Haiti and the Dominican Republic), and Puerto Rico (PWER-toh REE-koh).

The smallest and easternmost of the Greater Antilles, the island of Puerto Rico is 1,050 miles from Miami, Florida, and 550 miles from Caracas, Venezuela. Called the "Key to the Indies" and the "Crossroads of the Caribbean," Puerto Rico dominates one of the main entrances from the Atlantic Ocean to the Caribbean Sea. The island is bounded on the north by the Atlantic Ocean, and on the south by the Caribbean Sea.

A small rectangular-shaped island, Puerto Rico is about 100 miles long and 35 miles wide. Its lush green countryside and sandy beaches make Puerto Rico one of the most beautiful islands of the West Indies. Blessed with rich soil, a warm climate, and plenty of sunshine and rain, Puerto Rico abounds with tropical flowers and fruit-bearing trees. It is not surprising, then, that the national anthem of Puerto Rico describes the island as a "flowering garden of magical beauty."

PART I

The Early History of Puerto Rico

1. *The First Inhabitants: The Arawak Indians*

The first inhabitants of Puerto Rico were the Arawak Indians. These short, copper-colored natives of South America journeyed from Venezuela to Puerto Rico about 2,000 years ago. Since it is possible that North and South America were connected by land at this time, there is no way of knowing whether the Arawaks traveled by land or by sea. It is certain, however, they came to Puerto Rico in small numbers, and over a long period of time.

The Arawaks named their new home *Boriquén* (boh-ree-KEN), or "Fatherland of Valiant Men." Because Boriquén was a land of plenty, the Arawak Indians enjoyed a comfortable, easygoing existence there. While the men spent their time fishing and hunting, the women gathered berries, pineapples, and other tropical fruits. The Arawaks also farmed on a limited basis, planting corn, peanuts, sweet potatoes, and a number of other crops.

The small tribal villages of the Arawaks were usually located in the valleys, close to the agricultural fields. Most of the villages consisted of simple huts built on either side of a dirt road. The largest hut always belonged to the *cacique* (KA-see-kay), or chief. The cacique governed all tribal affairs, and his word was law.

An Arawak artisan fashioned this
clay head in about 1200 A.D.

The Arawak Indians believed that spirits or gods controlled
everything in nature, including plants and animals, the earth and
the sky, the sun and the rain. In order to please these gods, the
Arawaks honored them with sacred rites and offerings. One god
that the Arawaks could not please, however, was Huracán, the
god of evil. Feared and hated more than any other deity, Huracán
brought terrible winds to the island every fall (today, these winds
are called "hurricanes").

Although not as grave a threat as Huracán, the fierce Carib
Indians who inhabited the islands to the south and east of Boriquén were also feared by the Arawaks. The Caribs were a bold,
seafaring people, and they attacked Boriquén frequently, taking
many captives. While the more fortunate captives were enslaved
by the Caribs, the less fortunate ones were eaten by them. The
Arawak Indians were not fond of warfare, but they soon learned
to protect themselves from the cannibalistic savages who gave
their name to the Caribbean Sea.

For centuries, the fierce Carib Indians plagued the island of Puerto Rico. This 17th-century engraving shows the Caribs attacking Spanish ships.

2. *Boriquén Becomes a Spanish Colony*

On September 23, 1493, Christopher Columbus left Spain and set out on his second voyage to the New World. Commanding a fleet of 17 ships, Columbus set his course for Hispaniola, the West Indies island he had discovered on his first voyage. Early in November, Columbus stopped at the small Caribbean island of Guadeloupe for water. While exploring the island, he met several Arawak Indians who had been taken from the neighboring island of Boriquén and enslaved by the Carib Indians. The Arawaks begged Columbus to take them home to Boriquén, and Columbus agreed.

The Spanish fleet reached the beautiful green island of Boriquén on November 19, 1493. Impressed with the island, Columbus took possession of it in the name of Ferdinand and Isabella, the rulers of Spain. He named the island San Juan Bautista, after

Saint John the Baptist. Columbus also gave the Arawak Indians a new name. Because *taíno*, an Indian word meaning "peace," was the first word the Arawaks spoke to Columbus, he called them *Taínos*. After a three-day stop at the island, Columbus and his fleet left to continue their voyage to Hispaniola.

For 15 years the island of San Juan Bautista was ignored by Spain. But in 1508 a Spanish nobleman, Ponce de León, was sent with 50 men to explore the island. On the north coast of the island, Ponce de León discovered a large well-protected bay. Upon viewing the bay, he exclaimed, "Ay, que puerto rico!" ("Oh, what a rich port!"). In time, the whole island became known as Puerto Rico, while the port itself became known as San Juan—a shortened version of the island's former name.

When Ponce de León and his men landed on the island, they were received well by the friendly Arawak Indians. In their bright armor and glittering helmets, the Spaniards seemed like gods to the Indians. As a gesture of friendship and peace, the great Arawak chief Agüeybana exchanged names with Ponce de

Christopher Columbus, the discoverer of Puerto Rico, with a globe showing the New World

León, thereby making the Spaniard his son. Unfortunately, Ponce de León and his men were more interested in the chief's gold necklace than in his friendship. When they asked him where the gold came from, the chief told them that the streams of the Yauco River were rich with it. After visiting the streams for themselves, the Spaniards had all they could do to contain their delight at finding gold.

In 1509 Ponce de León began the first Spanish settlement in Puerto Rico. That same year he was made the first governor of the island. Since the Arawak Indians believed that the Spaniards were gods sent from the land of immortals, they peacefully submitted to their authority. Taking advantage of the Indians' peaceful nature, the Spaniards enslaved them and seized their lands. In return for laboring in the gold mines and farms of their Spanish masters, the Arawaks were offered instruction in the Christian faith and the Spanish culture.

Ponce de León became the first governor of Puerto Rico in 1509.

Instead of treating the friendly Arawak Indians
as equals, Spanish soldiers beat them into slavery.

The Arawak Indians believed that by cooperating with the Spaniards, they would eventually win their freedom back. But this was not the case. Poorly suited for the forced labor in the mines and fields, many of the Indians died of exhaustion and mistreatment. Others died of diseases brought to the island by the Spaniards. In 1511, after their pleas for better treatment were ignored, the Indians rebelled (they had seen Spaniards die, so they no longer looked upon them as gods). Enraged, Ponce de León and an army of 120 Spaniards ruthlessly shot down over 6,000 of the natives. Many of the Indians who were not killed fled to the mountains and to neighboring islands.

Convinced that the Arawak Indians were useless as workers, Ponce de León begged Ferdinand V, King of Spain, for permission to bring African slaves to Puerto Rico. Permission was granted, and in 1511 the first shipload of black slaves arrived at the island.

Still one of Puerto Rico's most important crops,
sugar cane was first brought to the island in 1515.

With the slaves came a terrible epidemic of smallpox that wiped out over one-third of the dwindling Arawak population. By 1515, less than 4,000 of the original 40,000 Arawak Indians remained on the island. Following another plague in 1519, their numbers were further reduced. Many of the Indians survived in the mountains and in neighboring islands, however, and they eventually intermarried with the Spaniards and Africans.

By the 1530s, Puerto Rico had been stripped of nearly all her gold. As a result, the Spaniards turned to agriculture for their livelihood. Sugar cane, which had been brought to Puerto Rico from Hispaniola in 1515, soon became the island's most important crop. In time, a number of small sugar mills were operating on the island.

Although the sugar cane offered Puerto Rico some hope of economic survival, the island was beset with problems throughout the 16th century. Resentful of the harsh treatment they received, the African slaves attempted many unsuccessful rebellions (as for the Arawak slaves, the few that remained were freed by Charles V of Spain in 1542). In addition to the slave uprisings, the island was plagued with devastating hurricanes, serious outbreaks of smallpox and other diseases, frequent raids by the Carib Indians, and numerous attacks by French, Dutch, and English pirates.

Recognizing the strategic importance of Puerto Rico as the gateway to the West Indies, Spain began converting the island into a military outpost during the 16th century. Spain was particularly eager to protect the port of San Juan because Spanish ships carrying the gold of Peru and the silver of Mexico always stopped there on the way home. So in 1533 work began on San Juan's first fortress, La Fortaleza. Six years later construction began on El Morro, the largest fortress in San Juan. Situated on the rocky tip of land overlooking the narrow entrance to the harbor,

An aerial view of El Morro, the mighty fortress
built by the Spaniards to protect San Juan Harbor

El Morro was built with towering 140-foot walls. Since the powerful guns of the fortress could be pointed at every approach to the harbor, Spain was confident of San Juan's ability to protect herself. But just to make sure, Spain installed a permanent garrison at El Morro in 1586.

El Morro's first important test came in 1595. That year Sir Francis Drake attacked San Juan in an attempt to win it for England. But El Morro's mighty guns blasted the English ships, killing over 500 of Drake's men. After three days of fighting, Drake and his fleet fled the island in defeat. Three years later, San Juan was attacked by another Englishman — George Clifford, the Earl of Cumberland. Rather than attempt to land at San Juan's well-protected harbor, Clifford landed his fleet on a spot several miles to the east of the harbor. With 1,000 troops, Clifford marched to San Juan, forced the surrender of El Morro, and captured the city. But five months later, a terrible epidemic of dysentery drove Clifford and his men from the island, and they never returned.

In 1625 Puerto Rico came dangerously close to falling into the hands of the Dutch. With an expedition of 17 ships and 2,500 men, Captain Bowdoin Hendrick sailed directly into San Juan Harbor and took possession of the city. But after three weeks of fighting, the Dutch forces still had not won control of El Morro. Enraged, Hendrick told the Spaniards he would burn San Juan to the ground if they did not surrender the fortress. When the Spaniards responded by continuing their attack on the Dutch, Hendrick set fire to the city and departed. El Morro was left undefeated, but the city it was built to protect lay in ruin.

In order to prevent anyone from ever capturing San Juan again, Spain decided to build a huge wall around the city. Finished in the 1650s, the massive wall was 25 feet high and 18 feet thick. Since it was guarded by three fortresses (El Morro foremost among them), the great wall of San Juan made the city almost unconquerable.

The Spanish governor of Puerto Rico (left) talks to an aid (right), while Dutch forces leave San Juan Harbor in defeat.

With the exception of Hendrick's attack in 1625, the 17th century was a relatively peaceful period in Puerto Rico's history. Since Spain was more concerned with the island's military role than with its economy, she did not establish huge slave-run plantations on the island. As a result, Puerto Rico was one of the only islands in the Caribbean whose white population far outnumbered its black. And since the Spaniards had learned to treat their Negro slaves better than they had treated the Arawak Indians, the slaves no longer rebelled against them. In fact, slaves were treated so well in Puerto Rico that many runaway slaves from British colonies in the Caribbean came to the island to seek refuge. Not wishing to enslave those asking for his protection, the king of Spain declared the runaway slaves free men.

By the end of the 17th century, many people were living in the interior of Puerto Rico. Others were living in small mountain villages or in secluded areas along the coast. Many of these people were a mixture of three racial-cultural groups: Indian, Spanish, and African. In fact, it was from the mixture of these three diverse groups that the Puerto Rican people gradually evolved. In San Juan, where intermarriage had always been popular (partly because of the shortage of Spanish women), Spanish-Indian and Spanish-African people were becoming quite common.

Although Puerto Rico was forbidden by royal decree to trade with any country except Spain until the 19th century, the only place on the island where the ban on foreign trade was actually enforced was San Juan. In the more remote areas along the island's coast, Puerto Rican farmers secretly traded with French, Dutch, and English ships. This illegal trade continued throughout the 17th and 18th centuries.

During the 18th century, Puerto Rico was allowed to export more goods to Spain than ever before. Naturally, this stimulated agricultural production on the island. Coffee, which was brought to Puerto Rico in 1736, soon became the island's most important crop. Sugar and tobacco—the traditional crops of Puerto Rico— were also raised, but on a much larger scale than in the past. Although this great expansion in Puerto Rico's agricultural production brought more slaves to the island, the slaves never comprised more than 10 percent of the island's population.

The agricultural boom in Puerto Rico strengthened the island's economy and stimulated a rapid growth in its population. The population rose from 45,000 in 1765 to 103,000 in 1787 to 150,000 in 1800. (Of the 150,000 people living in Puerto Rico in 1800, five out of every ten were Spanish, three were of mixed blood, one was a free Negro, and one was an enslaved Negro.) As Puerto Rico's population grew, the island gained a number of new towns. In 1690, the island had only five towns; by 1800, it claimed over 30.

With the close of the 18th century came the last major English attack on San Juan. In 1796, Spain and France jointly declared war on their common foe, England. In response, England sent a fleet of 60 ships to invade the Caribbean and to capture Spain's colonies. Since England had recently lost her American colonies, it was vital to her status as a world power that she win control of Spain's holdings in the New World.

Under the command of General Ralph Abercromby, the English fleet captured the island of Trinidad with very little effort. Victorious, the English fleet headed for Puerto Rico in April 1797. Since San Juan was now protected by a great wall and by several fortresses, Abercromby landed to the east of the city just as George Clifford had done 100 years earlier. The Puerto Ricans were determined to defend their city from the English, and they gathered a fighting force of over 6,500 men. Even *jíbaros*, or farmers, came down from the hills in San Juan's defense. Although Abercromby had over 7,000 troops, he was unable to break the defenses of the Puerto Ricans. So after a month of unsuccessful attacks on San Juan, the English fleet limped away from Puerto Rico in defeat. By repelling the English, the Puerto Ricans had proved that their island was indeed a "Fatherland of Valiant Men."

General Ralph Abercromby

3. *The Movement toward Autonomy*

The 19th century was a period of great political unrest for Puerto Rico. During the three previous centuries, the island had been ruled by a Spanish governor whose authority was absolute. All high government posts, in fact, had been filled by Spaniards. The Puerto Ricans had virtually no political rights, and the only country they were permitted to trade with was Spain.

With the opening of the 19th century, the people of Puerto Rico began to clamor for greater freedom. Unfortunately, Spain was too involved with her own political problems to deal effectively with those of Puerto Rico. The Spanish government underwent several upheavals during the 19th century, moving from monarchies to republics and back again to monarchies. As a result, its policies regarding Puerto Rico swung back and forth like a pendulum. Over and over again, Puerto Rico was invited to send representatives to the Spanish *Cortes*, or parliament. Each time, Spain promised her loyal colony legislative reforms that would give the island a greater degree of freedom and self-rule. And each time, Spain failed to keep her promises. Although Puerto Rico did enjoy some very brief periods of increased political freedom, these periods were followed by long stretches of absolute rule by Spanish governors. To the Puerto Ricans, it seemed as if their island was destined to remain a tightly controlled colony of Spain forever.

Puerto Rico's only major step forward during the first half of the 19th century was in the area of foreign trade. In 1810 Ramón Power, acting as Puerto Rico's first representative to the Spanish Cortes, vehemently attacked Spain's rigid trade policies. Five years later, in 1815, King Ferdinand VII issued the *Cédula de Gracias*, or Decree of Grace. Among other things, this important decree opened Puerto Rico's ports to the commerce of all nations. The long-awaited decree proved to be a catalyst to both the

In 1868 **Ramón Emeterio Betances** and a group of armed followers tried unsuccessfully to win independence for Puerto Rico.

economy and the population of Puerto Rico (by 1900, the island's population had risen to almost a million).

Fifty years after the Decree of Grace was passed, Puerto Rico's pleas for greater political freedom and independence had still not been answered. Tired of waiting for Spain to act, a radical group of Puerto Ricans decided to take matters into their own hands. The leader of the group, Ramón Emeterio Betances, felt that the time had come to declare Puerto Rico's independence from Spain. So on September 23, 1868, he and 400 armed followers marched into the small mountain town of Lares and captured the town hall. Raising banners with the words "Liberty or Death!" Ramón Emeterio* and his men proclaimed the birth of the Republic of Puerto Rico. Called *El Grito de Lares* ("The

---

*It is a Spanish tradition for children to use both their father's and mother's last names, in that order. But when only one surname is used, it is always the father's. Hence Ramon Emeterio Betances would be called Ramon Emeterio, but never Ramon Betances.

Cry of Lares"), the one-day uprising did not have popular support and was quickly put down. Its flag, however, was later adopted as the official flag of Puerto Rico.

In the years following the unsuccessful armed revolution of 1868, a strong movement for self-government arose in Puerto Rico. Spain abolished slavery in 1873, but this reform was not enough to satisfy Puerto Ricans who longed for self-rule. So in 1887 a group of Puerto Rican liberals held a peaceful assembly of protest at the city of Ponce. Although the assembly declared its loyalty to Spain, it demanded self-rule for Puerto Rico.

In response to the assembly, the Spanish governor of Puerto Rico initiated a reign of terror in which all known liberals were hunted down and imprisoned. Instead of dissolving Puerto Rico's movement for self-government, the violent attacks strengthened the movement. Within months of the 1887 assembly, the *Partido Unionista*, or Autonomy Party, was formed. As its name indicated, the object of this party was to secure political autonomy, or self-rule, for Puerto Rico.

In 1891, Luis Muñoz Rivera became the leader of the Autonomy Party. While some Puerto Ricans wanted to revolt against Spain and win complete independence for Puerto Rico, Luis Muñoz wanted to secure self-rule (not independence) for the island through peaceful, nonviolent means. When Cuba—Spain's only remaining colony in the New World besides Puerto Rico— revolted in 1895, Muñoz Rivera feared that Puerto Rico might take a similar course of action. So in 1896 he went to Spain to urge a grant of autonomy for the island. Práxedes Sagasta, the head of Spain's Liberal Party, promised that when his party gained control in Spain, self-rule would be granted to Puerto Rico.

When the Liberal Party came to power in 1897, Sagasta became Prime Minister of Spain. Just as he had promised, Sagasta granted Puerto Rico a Charter of Autonomy. In addition to giving Puerto Rico representation in the Spanish Cortes, the charter allowed the Puerto Ricans to elect most of their own government officials. More importantly, it gave Puerto Rico a two-chamber parliament, which consisted of a Chamber of Representatives and a Council of Administration. When a six-man executive cabinet was formed in Puerto Rico, Luis Muñoz Rivera was chosen as its leader. Since Muñoz Rivera was the first leader of the Puerto Rican government, he is often called the George Washington of Puerto Rico.

Unfortunately, self-rule did not last long in Puerto Rico; less than a year after the Charter of Autonomy was granted, the island fell under the control of a country even more powerful than Spain. So ended 400 years of Spanish domination, and so ended Puerto Rico's hard-won right to govern itself.

The executive cabinet of Puerto Rico's brief autonomous government of 1897. Seated, left to right: **Luis Muñoz Rivera, Francisco Quiñones, Manuel Fernandez Juncos**. Standing, left to right: **Juan Hernandez Lopez, José Sepero Quiñones, Manuel F. Rossy**.

PART II

From Colony to Commonwealth

1. *Puerto Rico Becomes a U.S. Possession*

When Cuba began her final revolt against Spain in 1895, most Americans sympathized with her cause. So in 1898, when it became clear that Cuba needed help to win her independence, the United States intervened and declared war on Spain. After freeing Cuba from Spanish control in July 1898, American forces headed for Puerto Rico. On July 25, 1898, General Nelson A. Miles landed on the southwest coast of the island with a force of 3,500 men. Because most Puerto Ricans hoped that America would insure democracy and prosperity for their island, they put up very little opposition to the American invasion.

On October 18, 1898, President William McKinley made General John R. Brooke the first American military governor of Puerto Rico. With Brooke's installation as the new governor of Puerto Rico, Spain's flag at El Morro was replaced by the Stars and Stripes. Having lost the Spanish-American War, Spain signed the Treaty of Paris on December 10, 1898, and officially ceded Puerto Rico to the United States.

The military government established on the island lasted until 1900. Although it deprived the Puerto Ricans of self-rule, it nevertheless improved the island's sanitation facilities, established an educational system, and built many highways, railroads, hospitals, and other public works. By and large, the two-year period of military government was a peaceful and productive

General Nelson A. Miles   General John R. Brooke

time in Puerto Rico's history. (The Puerto Ricans did suffer one insult during this period, however: their island was mistakenly called "Porto" Rico on all official U.S. documents, and the error continued well into the 1930s.)

In 1900 the U.S. Congress gave Puerto Rico some measure of self-rule by passing the first Organic Act, or the Foraker Act. This act replaced the island's military government with a two-house civil government. While the U.S. President retained the right to appoint the governor, his cabinet, and the upper legislative body, the Puerto Ricans were allowed to elect the lower legislature, as well as a Resident Commissioner in Washington D.C. The Resident Commissioner could speak to the U.S. Congress on Puerto Rican affairs, but he had no vote. Although the Foraker Act failed to give U.S. citizenship to Puerto Ricans, it exempted them from federal taxes. It also established free trade between the island and the United States—another point to Puerto Rico's advantage.

Puerto Rican patriot
Luis Muñoz Rivera

The Foraker Act gave Puerto Rico a civil government, but it left the island's political status in serious doubt: Puerto Rico was not an independent nation, nor a colony, nor an autonomous commonwealth, nor a state in the American union. The Foraker Act specified only that Puerto Rico was a U.S. possession—nothing more and nothing less.

Dissatisfied with Puerto Rico's uncertain status under the Foraker Act, Luis Muñoz Rivera went to Washington, D.C. in 1910 as the Resident Commissioner of his island. Accompanying Muñoz Rivera was his 12-year-old son, who one day would carry on his father's work. After arriving in Washington, Muñoz Rivera began his long crusade to win from the United States what he had won from Spain over 10 years earlier—autonomy for Puerto Rico. His tireless struggle paid off, for in 1917 the U.S. Congress passed the second Organic Act, or the Jones Act. This act defined Puerto Rico as an "organized but unincorporated" territory of the United States and made the Puerto Ricans citizens of the United States. Although it maintained the right of the U.S. President to appoint the governor of Puerto Rico, it gave the islanders the right to elect *both* houses of their government. The Jones Act did not give autonomy to Puerto Rico, but it was nevertheless a triumph for the island and for the island's greatest crusader— Luis Muñoz Rivera. Unfortunately, this great patriot died before the Jones Act could be put into effect.

From 1900 to 1925, the advancement of Puerto Rico's economy paralleled that of the island's political status. This period of great economic expansion in Puerto Rico was due partly to the increased trade with the United States and partly to U.S. government spending. But more important to the island's economy were U.S. businessmen. Since the island was a territory of the United States, no duty, or tax, had to be paid on exports and imports moving back and forth between Puerto Rico and the United States. Encouraged by this tariff protection, many American manufacturers moved their businesses to the island. More importantly, American businessmen invested in Puerto Rico's rich agricultural land, buying up small sugar fields from jíbaros and converting them into a few giant corporations.

As sugar production soared, the Puerto Rican economy was given a dramatic boost. Reflecting the expanding economy was an expanding population: during the 25-year period between 1900 and 1925, the population rose from about 1 million people to well over 2 million. By 1925, Puerto Rico's fantastic birth rate was quickly making the once-uninhabited island one of the most densely populated areas in the world.

Unfortunately, the economic expansion in Puerto Rico was short lived. American sugar corporations continued to make tremendous profits, but these profits went to the wealthy investors in the United States—*not* to the poor Puerto Rican jíbaros who slaved long hours in the fields and mills. On the whole, the jíbaros were paid very low wages—sometimes less than 50 cents a day. And since the work was seasonal (the "dead season" stretched from June to November, while the cane was growing), many Puerto Ricans were out of work for long periods of time.

While American sugar corporations were making huge profits in Puerto Rico, Puerto Rican sugar workers were laboring long hours for very low wages.

Thus, by converting Puerto Rico's economy into a one-crop economy, American businessmen made the vast majority of Puerto Ricans dependent on a business that could only employ them on a part-time basis.

Two devastating hurricanes — one in 1928 and one in 1930 — left the island's economy in an even worse state than before. While the American-owned sugar corporations continued to make money, the working class people of Puerto Rico plunged into a helpless state of poverty. Unemployment increased greatly, along with hunger, poor housing, disease, and the infant mortality rate. As the terrible depression years of the 1930s descended upon the island (and upon the United States), Puerto Rico's poverty-stricken state earned the island yet another new name: the "Poorhouse of the Caribbean."

When President Franklin D. Roosevelt came to office in 1933, he set up relief and reconstruction agencies for Puerto Rico similar to the agencies that were helping depression victims in the United States. The Puerto Ricans were U.S. citizens, after all, and they desperately needed the government's help. So in 1933 Roosevelt established the Puerto Rico Emergency Relief Administration, or PRERA. During its two-year life, this organization spent millions of dollars on food, clothing, and training programs for the Puerto Ricans. In a very real way, PRERA kept the population of Puerto Rico alive.

In 1935 Roosevelt established another organization to aid the islanders—the Puerto Rico Reconstruction Administration, or PRRA. This organization was aimed primarily at establishing new industries in Puerto Rico so that the island's economy would not be solely dependent upon agriculture. In addition to starting shoe and garment industries on the island, PRRA gave Puerto Rican farmers the right to buy back their land from one of the island's four giant sugar corporations.

Shortly after the creation of PRRA, Luis Muñoz Marín, the son of patriot Luis Muñoz Rivera, emerged as Puerto Rico's newest and most dynamic political leader. In 1938 he and his followers formed a progressive new party called *Partido Popular Democratico* (Popular Democratic Party), or PPD. As the 1940 legislative elections in Puerto Rico neared, Muñoz Marín claimed that

Luis Muñoz Marín campaigning for the Popular Democratic Party, 1940

the political status of the island was not the real issue; rather, the state of the island's economy was the issue. With "Bread, Land, and Liberty" as its slogan, the Popular Democratic Party proposed sweeping economic and social reforms for the island. Muñoz Marín's appeal to the working classes proved successful, for the Popular Democratic Party succeeded in winning a slim but vital majority in Puerto Rico's Legislative Assembly.

Following his party's victory, Muñoz Marín initiated the miraculous economic development program that was to eventually lift Puerto Rico out of poverty. Called "Operation Bootstrap," the progressive program received extensive financial backing from the U.S. government. Among the aims of the organization were industrialization, improved health and education, slum clearance, agricultural expansion, and land redistribution (this goal was to be accomplished by breaking up the large sugar corporations and distributing the land to the jíbaros). Although it took many years, millions of dollars, and a lot of hard work to achieve these goals, they all were eventually realized.

Slum clearance was one of the major goals of Operation Bootstrap.

As a result of Operation Bootstrap, substandard housing in Puerto Rico was replaced with modern housing complexes.

Impressed with the reforms begun under Operation Bootstrap, the Puerto Ricans gave overwhelming support to Muñoz Marín and the Popular Democratic Party in the 1944 legislative elections. Three years later, the U.S. Congress passed a law that paved the way for an even greater victory for Muñoz Marín. In an amendment to the Jones Act, Congress at last gave the people of Puerto Rico the right to elect their own governor. When the 1948 elections were held in Puerto Rico, Luis Muñoz Marín became the first governor of Puerto Rico to be elected by the Puerto Ricans. January 2, 1949, the day of Muñoz Marín's inauguration, was a proud and historic day for the Puerto Ricans.

Following his inauguration, Governor Muñoz devoted himself to making Operation Bootstrap a success. World War II had thwarted the ambitious economic program, leaving Puerto Rico's economy in a very weakened condition. So in order to insure Operation Bootstrap's main goal of industrialization, Muñoz created *Fomento*, or the Economic Development Association. Designed to encourage American investors to establish industries in Puerto Rico, the agency was a tremendous success. As more

Fomento, or the Economic Development Association, helped make Puerto Rico an industrial society by encouraging American investors to establish industries like this chemical plant on the island.

and more businesses and factories were established on the island, Puerto Rico slowly made the transition from an agricultural to an industrial society.

Of course, the startling transformation of the island's economy did not occur overnight. Following World War II and through the 1950s, the economy experienced many growing pains and many setbacks. As a result, thousands of unemployed Puerto Ricans left the island and migrated to the United States in the hopes of finding work and making a better life for themselves. During the 1960s, however, as Puerto Rico's economy began to improve, the great Puerto Rican exodus to the United States ended.

2. *The Commonwealth of Puerto Rico Is Created*

In addition to his work on Operation Bootstrap, Governor Muñoz began a campaign to improve Puerto Rico's political status. During the 1940 elections, Muñoz had said that Puerto Rico's economy—*not* its status—was the issue. But in 1949, as progress was being made on the island's economy, Muñoz Marín felt that the time had come to *make* an issue out of the political status of his homeland. While the Independent Party favored independence for Puerto Rico, and while the State Republican Party favored making the island a part of the United States, Governor Muñoz and the Popular Democratic Party wanted to make Puerto Rico a self-governing commonwealth. As such, the Puerto Ricans would govern their island and the United States would defend it. The people of Puerto Rico would remain U.S. citizens, but they would pay no federal taxes and have no vote in the national government.

On October 30, 1950, President Truman paved the way for making Puerto Rico a self-governing commonwealth by signing Public Law 600. While the 1947 amendment to the Jones Act had allowed the Puerto Ricans to elect their own governor, Public Law 600 gave them the right to draft their own constitution. In August 1951, the Puerto Ricans elected 92 delegates to their Constitutional Convention. Six months later the constitution was completed. Modeled after the U.S. Constitution, it gave Puerto Rico self-government, but stated that the island would remain an associated commonwealth of the United States.

In the elections of 1952, the Puerto Ricans approved the constitution and reelected Muñoz Marín as their governor. Then, on July 25, 1952, the U.S. Congress approved the Puerto Rican constitution. The Free Associated State of Puerto Rico (*Estado Libre Asociado de Puerto Rico*), or the Commonwealth of Puerto Rico, as it came to be called, was at last a reality. As Constitution Day was proclaimed throughout the island, a proud Governor Muñoz raised Puerto Rico's flag next to the Stars and Stripes. A new era had begun in the history of Puerto Rico.

In 1964, 12 years after Puerto Rico became a commonwealth, Governor Muñoz announced that he would not seek a fifth term as governor of the island. He had been elected to the office four times—in 1948, 1952, 1956, and 1960—and he felt that the time had come for him to step down. When the 1964 elections were held, Roberto Sánchez Vilella emerged as the island's new

The official seal of the Commonwealth of Puerto Rico

governor. A member of PPD, Sánchez had been Muñoz Marín's
secretary of state for many years.

Although the Popular Democratic Party did well in the 1964
elections, rival parties favoring statehood for Puerto Rico did
better than ever before. Obviously, the movement for Puerto
Rican statehood was gaining momentum. As a result, the U.S.
Congress appointed a special commission to study Puerto Rico's
political status. In 1966, the commission suggested that the
Puerto Ricans should again vote on their status. When the plebiscite was held on July 23, 1967, the Puerto Ricans were given
three options to choose from: the continuation of the commonwealth, statehood, or independence. Over 60 percent of the
people voted for the continuation of the commonwealth, with
39 percent wanting statehood and less than 1 percent favoring
independence.

The statehood movement failed to win the plebiscite, but it
showed a surprising amount of strength. And the movement
gained even more strength in 1968, when Luis A. Ferré was
elected as governor of Puerto Rico. A member of the New Progressive Party, Governor Ferré favors statehood for Puerto Rico.
If Ferré succeeds in winning more popular support for the statehood movement, Puerto Rico eventually may become a member
of the United States. Only time will tell.

Governor Luis A. Ferré

Whether or not Puerto Rico's political status changes, the future of the island's economy will almost certainly be bright. Although Operation Bootstrap still has a long way to go, it has already accomplished miracles for Puerto Rico's economy. Fomento, one of the main agencies of Operation Bootstrap, has brought over 2,500 factories to Puerto Rico and promises to bring many more in the future. Thanks to Fomento and to the willingness of American investors to establish businesses in Puerto Rico, the island has succeeded in becoming an industrialized society. Thus the major goal of Operation Bootstrap has been achieved.

Industrialization has brought many benefits to the island, including increased employment, higher wages, better housing, and a greatly improved educational system (illiteracy has almost been banished on the island). All these improvements have enabled Puerto Rico's 3 million people to enjoy a higher standard of living than ever before. But perhaps the most dramatic consequence of the improved state of the island's economy is that Puerto Ricans are now living longer than ever before. In the 1930s, before Operation Bootstrap began, the average life expectancy of the Puerto Ricans was less than 40; by 1972, it has risen to over 70! Considering what the Puerto Ricans have accomplished—both politically and economically—the "Fatherland of Valiant Men" is indeed a fitting name for their homeland.

PART III

The Migration
to the U.S. Mainland

1. *The First Migrants to the Mainland*

Although the Puerto Ricans did not begin migrating to this country in large numbers until the 1920s, the Puerto Rican migration to the U.S. mainland actually began around the turn of the century. When Puerto Rico was annexed by the United States in 1898, it was in a sad state of affairs. The overpopulated island was plagued with an underdeveloped economy, massive unemployment, poverty, hunger, poor housing, and a high death rate (the average life expectancy for Puerto Ricans was only 32). In search of a better life, small groups of Puerto Ricans crossed the Atlantic Ocean in boats and journeyed to the U.S. mainland.

Merchant seamen, garment makers, college students, and cigar makers were among the first Puerto Ricans to arrive on the U.S. mainland. Although they came to this country in small numbers, their communities on the mainland gradually grew in size and importance. In 1910, there were about 1,500 Puerto Ricans living in this country; by 1920, there were over 7,000 in New York City alone. While most of the migrants settled in New York—the traditional port of entry for boats from Puerto Rico—others settled in Chicago, Boston, New Orleans, and Miami.

With the passage of the Jones Act in 1917, the Puerto Rican migration to this country increased dramatically. Since the Jones Act made the Puerto Ricans citizens of the United States by birth, the islanders had as much right to migrate to the U.S. mainland as citizens already living on the mainland had to migrate from one state to another. Thus the restrictive immigration laws that were passed in this country in 1921 and 1924 did not apply to the Puerto Ricans.

When World War I ended in 1918, Puerto Rico was in the midst of a terrible depression. Poverty and unemployment were chronic, and the population of the already-overpopulated island was growing at a faster rate than ever before (this, because of a rising birth rate and a falling death rate). As a result, thousands of Puerto Ricans exercised their right as U.S. citizens to migrate to the mainland, where the economy was thriving and where jobs were plentiful.

By 1930, over 53,000 Puerto Ricans were living on the U.S. mainland. Like the first Puerto Ricans who had come to this

The poor housing in Puerto Rico was one of the things that encouraged many islanders to migrate to the U.S. mainland.

country, most of those who came during the 1920s settled in New York City (in 1930, over 45,000 Puerto Ricans were living in this city). Here, they had no trouble finding work. Since the postwar immigration laws had greatly limited the admission of Europeans to this country, the Puerto Ricans found many openings in jobs for unskilled and semiskilled workers—jobs that had traditionally been filled by European immigrants. Thousands of Puerto Rican women entered the New York garment industry, while Puerto Rican men found work in factories and in the service industries, such as hospitals, hotels, restaurants, and laundries.

During the Great Depression, which began in 1929 and lasted well into the 1930s, the migration of the Puerto Ricans to the U.S. mainland slowed down considerably. Jobs were as scarce in America as they were in Puerto Rico, and most Puerto Ricans simply could not afford the price of the boat ticket to the mainland (the cost was more than the average Puerto Rican earned in a year). Yet, the Puerto Rican population on the U.S. mainland rose from 53,000 to 70,000 between 1930 and 1940.

The year 1939 saw the beginning of World War II, a war which all but halted the Puerto Rican migration to this country. Jobs were plentiful in America during the war, but submarine warfare in the Caribbean made it difficult and hazardous for Puerto Ricans to make the voyage to this country. Some did come, however, and they readily found work on the mainland.

2. The Greatest Era of the Migration

After World War II ended in 1945, the greatest and most important period of the Puerto Rican migration to the continental United States began. Three factors encouraged the exodus of Puerto Ricans to this country following the war. First, Puerto Rico's economy was still weak and underdeveloped. Operation Bootstrap had begun in 1940, but its ambitious goals for strengthening the island's economy were far from accomplished; the grave problems of overpopulation, underemployment, and poverty had yet to be solved. Second, a great many jobs for unskilled and semiskilled workers were available on the U.S. mainland. This huge surplus of jobs had been created during the war, when thousands of unskilled laborers in America left their jobs to work in defense plants and factories. When the war ended, they continued working in the factories, thereby leaving their former jobs unfilled. And third, air transportation expanded rapidly after the war, becoming an important means of travel. The expansion of commercial air travel meant that large numbers of Puerto Ricans could fly from San Juan to New York City in a

A group of Puerto Rican women trained in household work by the government of Puerto Rico arrive at Newark Airport in New Jersey, 1948.

The Net Puerto Rican Migration to the U.S. Mainland from 1945 to 1956

1945	13,000	1951	53,000
1946	40,000	1952	59,000
1947	25,000	1953	69,000
1948	33,000	1954	22,000
1949	26,000	1955	45,000
1950	35,000	1956	52,000

matter of hours, and at relatively low costs (some airlines advertised one-way fares as low as $50).

Drawn by the opportunities for employment on the mainland, thousands upon thousands of Puerto Ricans came to this country by plane, thereby beginning the first great airborne migration in history. Although some Puerto Ricans already living on the mainland returned to Puerto Rico, the number of islanders coming to the mainland was far greater. In 1945, the net Puerto Rican migration to this country was over 13,000; the next year, the net migration climbed to almost 40,000. Following the outbreak of the Korean War in 1950, even greater numbers of islanders came to the mainland, primarily because of the increased need for manpower created by the war. In 1953, the year in which the largest number of Puerto Ricans came to the mainland, the net migration was over 69,000. By 1955, about 675,000 Puerto Ricans were living in this country, with 500,000 of them concentrated in New York City.

Toward the end of the 1950s, as automation began reducing the number of jobs for unskilled laborers in this country, the migration of the Puerto Ricans slowed down markedly. Yet, 900,000 Puerto Ricans were living on the U.S. mainland in 1960. While the vast majority of the migrants were in New York, sizable Puerto Rican communities also existed in such states as

New Jersey, Connecticut, Massachusetts, Pennsylvania, Ohio, and Illinois (the second largest Puerto Rican community was in Chicago). Although some Puerto Rican communities were also established in Florida and California, most Puerto Ricans avoided settling in the South or the West; the South was forbidding because of the racial tension there, and the West was simply too remote for most Puerto Ricans.

Major Population Centers of the Puerto Ricans on the U.S. Mainland, 1970

California		Jersey City	15,500
San Francisco	20,500	Newark	45,000
		Paterson	25,500
Connecticut		Perth Amboy	12,500
Bridgeport	20,500		
Hartford	15,500	New York	
		New York City	1,000,000
Illinois		Rochester	10,500
Chicago	120,000		
		Ohio	
Indiana		Cleveland	15,000
Gary	5,500		
		Pennsylvania	
Massachusetts		Philadelphia	45,000
Boston	25,000		
		Wisconsin	
New Jersey		Milwaukee	7,000
Camden	8,000		
Hoboken	15,500		

The Puerto Ricans living in the East and the Midwest found work in industrial factories, canneries, garment centers, steel mills, and iron foundries. Those employed in the service industries worked as kitchen helpers, bellboys, dishwashers, busboys, and hospital orderlies. Some Puerto Ricans became civil servants (mail-carriers in particular), and others found careers in the armed forces.

Still other Puerto Ricans were employed on the mainland as contract farm workers. When Puerto Rico's sugar season ended in June, thousands of Puerto Rican sugar workers signed contracts with mainland farm employers to come to this country and work in the agricultural fields of the northeastern states. In order to

Thousands of contract farm workers come from
Puerto Rico to work in this country each year.

protect the migrant workers from unfair treatment, the Commonwealth of Puerto Rico passed laws in 1947 and 1948 stating that
the contracts offered by mainland employers had to be approved
by Puerto Rico's Department of Labor. The contract farm worker
program is still operating, with about 20,000 Puerto Rican farm
workers migrating to this country each year. Of the thousands
who come each year, about 10 percent remain on the mainland.

3. The Migration Levels Off

In the 1960s, the Puerto Rican migration to the U.S. mainland
began to level off, primarily for three reasons. First, jobs for
unskilled workers were becoming increasingly scarce on the
mainland, and the volume of the Puerto Rican migration had
always been directly related to the volume of jobs in this country.
Second, the goals of Operation Bootstrap were finally being
realized in Puerto Rico. As more and more industries were established on the island, unemployment began to drop and the standard of living began to rise. Thus the islanders had less need of
migrating to the mainland.

A third reason for the leveling off of the Puerto Rican migration to the U.S. mainland was the temporary nature of the migration. The European immigrants of earlier years had made the long journey to this country by boat and had come with the intention of staying. Most of the Puerto Ricans, on the other hand, migrated to this country during the aviation age, when airplanes could take them to the U.S. mainland in a matter of hours. Many of them believed that their real roots were still in Puerto Rico and that one day, they would return to the island for good. While some of these people did eventually return to live in Puerto Rico, others continued to live in this country but made frequent trips back to the island. Since the price of an airplane ticket from New York to San Juan was relatively inexpensive, it was much easier for the Puerto Ricans to return to their homeland than it was for other ethnic groups in America to return to theirs.

In the 1960s then, there were several years in which more

Puerto Rican industries like this aluminum plant have provided many Puerto Ricans with jobs. As a result, fewer and fewer of the islanders are migrating to the mainland in search of work.

Puerto Ricans returned to the island than came to the mainland. In 1963, for example, 5,000 more Puerto Ricans migrated to the island than to the mainland. Nevertheless, the population of the Puerto Ricans on the U.S. mainland increased steadily through the 1960s. This growth in population stemmed *not* from the arrival of more migrants on the mainland, but rather from the high birth rates of the Puerto Ricans already living in this country.

During the 10-year period from 1960 to 1970, the Puerto Rican population of the continental United States grew from 900,000 to 1.5 million. In 1972, 1.8 million Puerto Ricans were living in this country—about half as many as were living on the island of Puerto Rico. That same year, New York City claimed over 1 million Puerto Ricans, or about 100,000 more than were living in San Juan, the capital of Puerto Rico.

Puerto Ricans on the U.S. Mainland at 10-Year Intervals

	U.S. MAINLAND	NEW YORK CITY
1910	1,500	500
1920	not available	7,000
1930	53,000	45,000
1940	70,000	61,000
1950	300,000	187,000
1960	900,000	630,000
1970	1,500,000	1,000,000

Thousands of Puerto Ricans continue to arrive on the mainland each year. But at the same time, thousands of Puerto Ricans living on the mainland return to the island. Thus the net migration of the Puerto Ricans to this country is very small. As the Puerto Rican families on the mainland (especially in cities like New York and Chicago) continue to grow in size, however, the Puerto Ricans are becoming an increasingly visible minority in America.

PART IV

The Puerto Rican Experience on the Mainland

1. *The Land of Plenty*

With the end of World War II and the advent of commercial airplane service, the greatest era of the Puerto Rican migration to this country began. Filled with the hope of finding a better life, thousands of Puerto Ricans made the plane trip from San Juan to New York. As they stepped off the planes at New York City's LaGuardia Airport, most of the newcomers carried cardboard suitcases that held everything they owned. Although the migrants were poor, they were confident that on the mainland — the land of opportunity — their fortunes would soon change.

Unlike the European immigrants who had come before them, the Puerto Ricans were U.S. citizens before they ever set foot on the mainland. *Like* earlier immigrants, however, they were faced with the problem of language. Spanish was the official language of Puerto Rico, and very few of the islanders who came to the U.S. mainland understood English. Few of those who came to this country during the winter months understood New York's frigid climate either; snow was something most Puerto Ricans had only seen in movies.

In spite of the language barrier and the cold, the Puerto Rican migrants were glad to be on the U.S. mainland. Since they were usually met at the airports by friends and relatives who had come to this country before them, the newcomers felt almost at home on the mainland. As mentioned earlier, the great majority of the migrants settled in New York City. In most cases, they stayed with relatives until finding work. While they were looking for

Most of the Puerto Ricans who migrated to the mainland settled in New York City.

jobs, they quickly learned to find their way around the towering city they had heard and read so much about. New York was cold and forbidding in many ways, but still, it was one of the most exciting cities in the world.

2. *The Land of Problems*

Between 1945 and the early 1950s, jobs for unskilled and semiskilled laborers were plentiful in this country—especially in large cities like New York. Thus the Puerto Ricans who came to the mainland during the postwar period had no problems finding work in factories and in the service industries. These jobs provided the migrants with a steady income—something they had never known in Puerto Rico. But at the same time, they were the lowest paying and least desirable jobs on the mainland. And because most of the Puerto Ricans did not speak or understand English, they had little chance of advancing to higher positions.

46

At first, the Puerto Ricans were grateful just to be employed, no matter how low their jobs were on the occupational totem pole; after all, they were making higher wages than they had ever made in Puerto Rico. But what they hadn't counted on was the high cost of living in New York. By the time they finished paying for food, clothing, transportation, and housing, they had little or no money left over. And as U.S. citizens living on the mainland, they were now subject to state and federal taxes—something else they hadn't counted on.

Thousands of the Puerto Ricans who came to this country between 1945 and the early 1950s took low-paying jobs as factory workers.

Since the Puerto Ricans filled the lowest paying occupations, they had little choice but to live in the poorest neighborhoods. For the Puerto Ricans who settled in New York, this meant living in the inner-city slums. The Puerto Ricans began concentrating in East Harlem, a slum on the east side of Manhattan, in the late 1920s. By the late 1940s, so many were living in the area that it became known as Spanish Harlem or *El Barrio*, which is Spanish for "The Neighborhood." Large numbers of Puerto Ricans settled in other areas of the city (notably the East Bronx),

Children play in a vacant lot between some run-down tenements in El Barrio.

but El Barrio was—and still is—the area most strongly identified with New York City's Puerto Rican population.

The housing in El Barrio and other Puerto Rican districts in New York City was overcrowded, high priced, and run down. In many cases, large families of seven or more people were crowded into tiny three-room apartments consisting of a combination living room-bedroom, a bathroom, and a kitchen. Less fortunate families lived in a single room, sharing a common bathroom and kitchen with several other families. Whether a three-room or a one-room apartment, the conditions were the same: cracked ceilings and walls, broken windows, faulty plumbing, poor heating (especially during the cold winter months), and rats.

Even with both parents working, most Puerto Rican families could not afford better housing. In fact, many couldn't even afford to live in the slums. As a result, they turned to city, state, and federal agencies for financial aid. Unlike the immigrants who had come to this country half a century earlier, the Puerto Ricans who came during and after the 1940s arrived at a time when welfare programs were fairly well established. In this respect, then, they were more fortunate than many of the earlier newcomers to the continental United States.

Poor jobs and poor housing were not the only problems the Puerto Ricans faced on the mainland. Another serious problem was that of racial prejudice and discrimination. Although thousands of Puerto Ricans had been living in New York City before World War II, they had been relatively unnoticed amid New York's millions of inhabitants. But after the war, as the Puerto Ricans poured into New York and became an increasingly visible minority, the prejudice against them mounted. By the late 1940s, the Puerto Rican migrants were widely known by the derogatory term "spic" (it is believed that this word was lifted from one of the most frequently spoken phrases of the migrants: "No spik Inglis").

Because of their poor English and their dark skins, the Puerto Ricans were discriminated against in jobs, in housing, and in the more "exclusive" hotels and restaurants. This sort of cruelty based upon color was very difficult for the migrants to understand because they came from a country where racial intermarriage was commonplace and where racial discrimination was practically nonexistent.

Color was not an issue in Puerto Rico, but it was a very hot issue in this country—especially with the beginning of the civil rights movement in the 1950s. And adding fuel to the prejudice against the Puerto Ricans (and the blacks, for that matter) was the fact that more and more of them were going on welfare. This was because many of the jobs for unskilled laborers that had been so plentiful immediately following the war were now being eliminated by automation.

Many people in this country accused the Puerto Ricans of coming here solely for the purpose of getting free handouts on the welfare programs. By and large, this was a cruel and unjust accusation. In fact, most Puerto Ricans considered it a terrible disgrace to be on welfare. Puerto Rican men took great pride in their work, so being unemployed and on welfare was a serious blow to their "machismo," or sense of manliness.

In sharp contrast to their secluded lives on the island, many Puerto Rican wives who migrated to the mainland took jobs outside the household.

The dignity and male pride of Puerto Rican men living on the mainland was also threatened by the elevated position of Puerto Rican women in this country. In Puerto Rico, a wife was expected to stay at home, take care of her children, and bow to the authority of her husband—the unquestioned head of the family. But on the mainland, Puerto Rican wives took jobs outside the household, did all the shopping, and dealt with teachers, doctors, and other outside agents.

Because of their strong sense of male pride, many Puerto Rican men resented the new freedom and independence of their wives on the mainland. Even more disturbing to them was the fact that their wives often earned higher wages than they did. But the final humiliation came when their wives were working and they were not. Having their wives support them and their families was more than some Puerto Rican men could accept. As a result, they left their families in disgrace. This, in part, explains the high rate of broken marriages among the Puerto Ricans in this country during the 1950s.

Other family problems also plagued the Puerto Rican migrants. Since they came from a country where children were expected to respect and obey their parents without question, Puerto Rican adults living on the mainland found it difficult to accept the parental permissiveness toward children in mainland society. On the other hand, Puerto Rican children in this country enjoyed their new-found freedom and rebelled against the old-world attitudes of their parents. This was particularly true of Puerto Rican girls. In Puerto Rico, they had been closely guarded and strictly chaperoned; on the mainland, they ventured outside their homes and engaged in a much freer social life than they had ever known before.

Another thing that broadened the gap between Puerto Rican parents and their children was the fact that in most cases, the children learned English much more rapidly than their parents did. Consequently, some Puerto Rican youths lost respect for their parents and began to act as they pleased.

Education was another of the problems faced by the Puerto Ricans who migrated to the mainland. Well-planned educational programs for the Puerto Ricans might have helped the migrants learn English and adjust to American culture. Unfortunately, no such programs existed. Because most of their teachers spoke only English, Puerto Rican children had a difficult time in school and performed very poorly. Humiliated and discouraged, many dropped out of school and looked for unskilled jobs that didn't require much education.

Unable to find work, many of the Puerto Rican youths who had left school banded together into gangs. Although these gangs eventually became involved in violence and bloodshed, they nevertheless served an important and worthwhile purpose. By joining a gang and wearing a jacket with the gang's insignia and name on it, young Puerto Rican men who had felt lost and defeated in New York gained a sense of solidarity and toughness. And adding to this sense of toughness was the fact that each gang ruled a special "turf," or territory, of its own.

While most Puerto Rican gangs were at first peaceful, they

This scene from *West Side Story* captures the tension between two opposing gangs in New York City.

became more and more warlike as they began to clash with opposing Italian and black gangs. When one gang dared to invade another gang's turf, a "rumble," or fight, erupted. During the 1950s, as the friction between opposing gangs mounted, gang warfare became a serious problem in New York City. (This problem was lyrically documented in Leonard Bernstein's stage musical *West Side Story*, which went on to become one of the most successful and highly acclaimed motion pictures of the sixties.)

3. *The Identity Crisis*

Gang fights, education, broken homes, discrimination, unemployment, poor housing, the language barrier—all these were serious problems for the Puerto Ricans who came to this country. But perhaps the most serious problem of all was that of the migrants' *identity*. Since many of the Puerto Ricans living on the mainland still looked upon Puerto Rico as their *real* home, they felt as if they did not really belong to or form a part of the mainland. And this feeling of "not belonging" was strengthened by the fact that as thousands of Puerto Ricans came to the mainland, thousands of others "returned home" to Puerto Rico.

The identity crisis of the Puerto Ricans was directly linked with the reluctance of the migrants to get involved in mainland politics—one channel through which they might have been able to solve many of the problems they faced in this country. As U.S. citizens living on the mainland, the Puerto Ricans had every right to participate in political activities and to vote in political elections. But since many of the migrants were determined to return to Puerto Rico as soon as they had "made good" on the mainland, they did not register to vote or engage in politics. As a result, they had no representatives in the city, state, and federal governments to fight for them or to help improve the quality of their lives on the mainland.

The failure of the Puerto Ricans to see themselves as permanent residents of the mainland also explains why they did not establish many community organizations in this country. Earlier immigrants from Europe had established such organizations to help the immigrants that followed them learn about and adjust to life in America. If the Puerto Ricans had done the same thing,

The flag of Puerto Rico. Because many of the Puerto Ricans who migrated to the mainland felt that they still owed their allegiance to the island, they did not see themselves as true residents of the mainland.

they might have gained a much stronger sense of identity and solidarity in this country.

Ironically, it was the Puerto Rican government—*not* the Puerto Rican migrants—that established the first important Puerto Rican organizations on the U.S. mainland. In order to help its people on the mainland, the Commonwealth of Puerto Rico set up migration offices in New York, New Jersey, Chicago, and other cities where large numbers of Puerto Ricans were living (this was the first time in history that a government crossed an ocean and followed its people to a new land). These Puerto Rican offices tried to make life on the mainland easier for the migrants by helping them find jobs and housing, by offering them free English lessons, and by protecting them against discrimination.

4. *Life in El Barrio*

Although the Puerto Rican migrants took little initiative in starting community organizations on the mainland, they *did* establish their own communities in New York and other large mainland cities. The most famous of these was, and is, El Barrio. Located in New York City's East Harlem district, The Neighborhood was overcrowded, dirty, and run down—it was a slum. But at the same time, it was distinctly Puerto Rican.

The streets of El Barrio were marked not only by dingy tenement buildings, but also by Puerto Rican movie houses showing Spanish-language films, by travel agencies offering "thrift" flights back to Puerto Rico, and by candy stores featuring jukeboxes that played Spanish records. Other landmarks of The Neighborhood included restaurants and bakeries, laundries and garment shops, dance halls and bars, and *bodegas*—small grocery stores selling fruits, vegetables, and other foods especially imported from Puerto Rico.

Sandwiched in between the many stores of the tightly packed neighborhood were a number of storefront churches, most of which were Protestant. Traditionally, the Puerto Ricans had been

A busy bodega in the heart of El Barrio

Roman Catholics (Catholicism was brought to Puerto Rico by the Spaniards during the 15th century). On the mainland, however, many Puerto Ricans fell away from the Catholic Church and joined the storefront churches established in El Barrio by such Protestant sects as the Baptists and the Pentecostals. These churches had small, tightly knit congregations, and they featured lively services with plenty of singing and clapping. Most important, the churches served a social function for the migrants by sponsoring recreation centers, athletic clubs, and other activities for them.

During New York's long cold winter, El Barrio's streets were nearly deserted. Most Puerto Ricans stayed indoors, venturing out into the forbidding cold only for work, school, and shopping. But when summer arrived, the streets of The Neighborhood were humming with activity. After hibernating in their stuffy apartments all winter long, the Puerto Ricans now lived on the streets. Jukeboxes and bands filled the air with the Latin music, and people gathered in front of their tenements for informal meetings and for sidewalk parties. While children played stickball and other street games, teenagers and young adults went to the dance halls to participate in dance contests and to listen to the jam sessions of competing local bands. Daily wedding processions also added to the color and excitement of El Barrio during the warm summer months.

More than colorful and exciting, El Barrio was, and is, one of the friendliest and most tightly knit communities in New York. The Puerto Ricans formed warm lasting friendships in El Barrio, and they usually shared what little they had with their friends and neighbors. No matter how poor they were, the Puerto Ricans never failed to open their doors and their hearts to hungry children and adults.

Puerto Rican children living in East Harlem play basketball on the sidewalk, putting the ball through the rungs of a fire-escape ladder.

This warmth and affection was most evident within the Puerto Rican families. Although some families did fall apart—either because of broken marriages or because of strained parent-child relations—most of the Puerto Rican families that came to this country remained together in spite of the problems they faced. In fact, the problems on the mainland often strengthened and solidified family bonds, bringing families closer together than ever before.

Love, laughter, and joy are shared on a summer day in El Barrio.

The families in El Barrio and other Puerto Rican districts on the mainland frequently lived with, or very close to, their relatives. Just as they shared their belongings with their friends and neighbors, so too, they shared whatever they had with their relatives. In many cases, relatives served as godparents to their brothers' and sisters' children. The godparent system was highly respected, and most Puerto Ricans treated their godchildren just as they treated their own children.

Life for the Puerto Ricans who came to New York and other mainland cities was not easy, but it wasn't all bad either. The jobs were low paying and undesirable, but at least they were jobs. The tenements were old and dingy, but they were better than no homes at all. The cities were cold and forbidding, but friends and families were always there to give warmth and comfort. If life on the mainland was not the best of all possible worlds, neither was it the worst.

PART V

Steps toward a Better Life on the Mainland

During the 1950s and 1960s, more and more Puerto Rican migrants began to look upon themselves as permanent residents of the U.S. mainland. They might still make occasional trips back to Puerto Rico to visit friends and relatives, but they regarded the mainland as their new home. This was especially true of the second-generation Puerto Ricans who were born in this country. To many of them, the U.S. mainland was their "heart place," while Puerto Rico remained secondary in their affection.

As the migrants became more certain of their identity—of their status as permanent residents of the U.S. mainland—they looked for ways to solve their problems and to improve the quality of their lives in this country. During the mid-1950s, a group of Puerto Ricans living in New York City established the Puerto Rican Forum, the first major Puerto Rican organization formed in this country by the migrants themselves. A Puerto Rican migration office was established in New York back in 1948, but it was organized by the government of Puerto Rico—*not* by the migrants themselves.

Representatives of the Puerto Rican Forum meet to discuss ways of strengthening Puerto Rican participation in economic affairs.

Still the most important and widely backed Puerto Rican organization in this country, the Puerto Rican Forum was established in order to give the Puerto Ricans of New York City a voice with which to air their problems and promote their interests. More importantly, the forum brought the migrants together for the first time, solidifying them as a group. Unified under one organization, New York City's Puerto Rican community was able to attack its problems and fight for improvements with greater power and strength than ever before.

An offshoot of the Puerto Rican Forum was the Puerto Rican Community Development Project. First funded by the Office of Economic Opportunity in 1965, this militant organization was established for the purpose of developing specific programs for the improvement of New York City's Puerto Rican community. Still very active, the organization has promoted a sense of identity, stability, and political strength among the Puerto Ricans of New York. It has been directly involved in job training programs, youth organizations, housing projects, drug-addiction programs, and voter registration drives. Although not all of the goals and demands of the very vocal and determined organization have been met, the Puerto Rican Community Development Project has achieved much.

Due partly to the influence of organizations like the Puerto Rican Community Development Project, and due partly to their growing sense of identity as mainland residents, the Puerto Ricans have come a long way in the area of politics. Before 1965, the Puerto Ricans living in New York and several other mainland cities were required to take a literacy test in English before registering to vote. Since most of the Puerto Ricans couldn't read

Community workers of the Puerto Rican Community Development Project help to register voters in the streets of East Harlem.

English, they failed the test and were denied the right to vote. This was terribly unjust because Spanish had remained the official language of Puerto Rico even after the island's people were made U.S. citizens in 1917.

When the Federal Voting Rights Act was passed by Congress in 1965, the discriminatory practice of forcing Puerto Ricans to take an English literacy test before voting was ended. The law stated that no U.S. citizen who had received an elementary school diploma in a country where the classroom language was other than English could be denied the right to vote. The Federal Voting Rights Act was a great victory for the Puerto Ricans in this country, and it allowed many of them to participate in mainland politics and government for the first time.

Today, *"Despierta Borriqua—defiende lo tuyo"* ("Wake up, Puerto Rican—defend what's yours") is a familiar phrase in Puerto Rican communities throughout this country. The "political awakening" of the Puerto Ricans is reflected by the fact that each year, more and more of them (especially second-generation Puerto Ricans) are registering to vote. By working "within the system," they are attempting to pass new laws and win new programs that will benefit the Puerto Rican community. Through their political activities, they are also trying to end discriminatory practices in housing, employment, and education.

Although the Puerto Ricans are newcomers to mainland politics, they have already made considerable progress in politics and government. In 1970 the Puerto Ricans living in the Bronx (one of the five boroughs of New York City) displayed their political strength by electing Herman Badillo to the U.S. House of Representatives. A Democrat, Badillo became the first Puerto Rican to be seated in the U.S. Congress. Just as John Kennedy's presidential victory in 1960 removed the prejudice against Catholics in government, Badillo's victory in 1970 helped remove the prejudice against Puerto Ricans in government.

In 1970 New York's Puerto Rican population claimed not only

Armando Montano

Manuel Ramos

one U.S. Congressman, but also four elected representatives in The New York State Government: Senator Roberto García and State Assemblymen Armando Montano, Luis Nine, and Manuel Ramos. In 1971 the Puerto Ricans also had three city commissioners in New York: Marta Valle, Commissioner of the Youth Services Agency; Joseph Rodríguez Erazo, Commissioner of the Manpower and Career Development Agency; and Amalia Betanzos, Commissioner of Relocation.

Amalia Betanzos

While most Puerto Ricans have tried to win political and social gains by supporting such conventional, nonviolent organizations as the Puerto Rican Forum in New York and the *Caballeros de San Juan* (the Knights of Saint John) in Chicago, some have supported more radical organizations, such as the Young Lords. This militant organization was established in 1968 by a group of young Puerto Rican radicals in New York's East Harlem district. Patterned after the Black Panthers, the Young Lords demand "Power to the People." Although the group has advocated violence as a means of winning concessions for the Puerto Rican community (it occupied an East Harlem church in the spring of 1970), it has also been involved in many peaceful projects. These projects include youth clubs, drug-addiction centers, breakfast programs for ghetto children, and health clinics.

Members of the Young Lords walk in a funeral procession through the streets of El Barrio. They carry a coffin bearing the body of a Young Lord who died in jail.

Since the 1950s, a number of Puerto Rican citizens' groups have been established in New York, Chicago, Boston, and other cities to fight for such nonpolitical goals as better housing and education. In New York, the East Harlem Tenants Council has convinced city officials to tear down some of El Barrio's worst tenements and replace them with modern housing complexes. The council has also succeeded in getting new playgrounds, parks, libraries, and health clinics for East Harlem. Another Puerto Rican group, the Emergency Tenants Council (ETC), has scored similar successes in Boston. In 1970, ETC organized a strike against a powerful tenement owner and legally forced him to bring his tenements up to city standards. The organization has also been involved in the city redevelopment project which began in Boston in 1969.

The Puerto Ricans living in this country have also made significant progress in the area of education. *Aspira*, the largest and most important educational organization of the Puerto Ricans, was established in New York during the early 1960s. The word *aspira* means "ambition," and Aspira's main goal has been to instill in school-age Puerto Ricans the ambition to finish high

Members of New York City's Board of Education visit CREO (Creating Resources for Educational Opportunity), a school established in East Harlem by Aspira.

This mobile language classroom is operated by BOLT (Basic Occupational Language Training), a program of the Puerto Rican Forum. The program is designed to help Puerto Ricans learn to speak English so that they can get good jobs.

school and enter college. Supported by the federal government and by leading Puerto Rican professionals and businessmen, the organization has set up vocational guidance programs, scholarship funds, English-tutoring programs, and youth clubs in junior and senior high schools throughout the nation.

Another encouraging sign for the Puerto Ricans is the fact that more and more school systems are setting up bilingual education programs for Spanish-speaking children. Under these programs, classes are conducted in both English and Spanish. The rise in bilingual education programs for Puerto Rican, Mexican, and Cuban children stems mainly from the federal Bilingual Education Act of 1968. To help "ensure equal educational opportunity to every child," the act has provided school systems with financial aid to initiate bilingual programs for the "large numbers of children of limited English-speaking ability in the United States." Since the passing of the Bilingual Education Act, bilingual school programs have been established in many states, including New York, Illinois, and Massachusetts (in Massachusetts, schools are required *by law* to have bilingual programs for children whose native language is other than English).

As the Puerto Ricans are becoming better educated, they are finding it easier to get jobs as skilled workers or as professionals. This is especially true of second-generation Puerto Ricans on the mainland, many of whom are becoming lawyers, doctors, teachers, social workers, electricians, plumbers, and businessmen. In 1972 the Puerto Rican Merchants Association, which aids and represents small businesses in New York, claimed well over 5,000 members. Among the Puerto Rican businesses represented by the organization are restaurants, grocery stores (or bodegas), newspapers, laundries, banks, bars, barbershops, and small factories.

Bodegas, restaurants, candy stores, and many other small businesses are represented by the Puerto Rican Merchants Association.

Many of the Puerto Rican businesses in New York City have received financial assistance from both the Puerto Rican Merchants Association and from the Small Business Administration — a federal agency that loans money to people who want to establish their own businesses. Two other federal agencies — the U.S. Office of Economic Opportunity and Job Corps — have helped many Puerto Ricans find work as unskilled or semiskilled laborers. The latter agency has been especially helpful to young Puerto

Raul Vasquez (left), who learned plumbing through the Job Corps, teaches the trade to other disadvantaged youths.

Ricans who have dropped out of school. Through Job Corps, many of the school dropouts have improved their English, earned the equivalent of a high school diploma, and learned a trade.

Although the Puerto Ricans have made important gains in politics, housing, education, and employment, it would be dishonest to imply that they have solved *all* of their problems. Many are still unemployed; many are still on welfare; many are still living in the slums; many are still dropping out of school; many are still unable to understand English. Yet, in spite of all these problems, the future of the Puerto Ricans in this country looks far brighter than it did 20, or even 10, years ago. Nearly 2 million Puerto Ricans are living on the U.S. mainland. If they continue to work together, they will succeed in making this country a better place to live—for themselves, and for all Americans.

PART VI

Individuals
and Their Achievements

Although the Puerto Ricans are latecomers to the U.S. mainland, they have already accomplished a great deal in this country. Through their achievements in government, business, literature, sports, and entertainment, they have made an important contribution to life on the U.S. mainland. Of course, many Puerto Ricans have also distinguished themselves on the island. But since the scope of this book is limited, only those Puerto Ricans living on the mainland will be discussed.

1. *Government*

As mentioned earlier, the Puerto Ricans have made considerable progress in the area of mainland politics and government. In New York, a number of Puerto Ricans have won positions as city and state officials. While Marta Valle, Joseph Rodríguez Erazo, and Amalia Betanzos have become city commissioners, Felipe N. Torres, Armando Montano, Luis Nine, and Manuel Ramos have become state assemblymen. More importantly, Roberto García has been elected to the New York State Senate, and Herman Badillo Rivera to the U.S. House of Representatives.

Roberto García has the distinction of being the first Puerto Rican to be elected to the New York State Senate. A native of the mainland, García was born in New York's Bronx in 1933. His career in politics began in 1965, when he was named as the congressional assistant to U.S. Congressman James A. Scheuer. After serving as a congressional assistant for two years, García was elected to the New York State Assembly. Then, in 1968, he ran as a candidate for state senator from New York's East Harlem -South Bronx District. In an overwhelming show of strength, García won over 45 percent of the votes, thereby becoming New York's first Puerto Rican state senator. Senator García has worked hard for the Puerto Rican community of New York, and he seems assured of being reelected for as long as he wishes to remain a state senator.

Roberto García

Like Roberto García, Herman Badillo has scored another "first" for the Puerto Ricans: he is the first to be seated in the U.S. Congress. Unlike García, Herman Badillo is a native of Puerto Rico. He was born in Caguas, a city near San Juan, in 1929. Badillo came to New York in 1941, shortly after the death of his parents. By working as a dishwasher, he managed to put himself through college and law school. Badillo graduated from the Brooklyn Law School in 1954 and became a practicing lawyer the following year.

Herman Badillo entered politics in 1961 in order to further the goals and interests of New York's Puerto Rican community. He received his first major government appointment one year later, when he was named Commissioner of the Department of Relocation. By seeing to it that Puerto Ricans who were moved from the slums were treated fairly and humanely, Badillo won the wide support of the Puerto Rican community. As a result, he was easily elected in 1965 as president of the Bronx Borough—an area that is heavily populated by Puerto Ricans.

Badillo resigned as borough president of the Bronx in 1969 in order to run as a Democratic candidate for mayor of New York City. Although Badillo lost the election to incumbent Mayor John Lindsay, he showed considerable support and finished a strong third in the election. When the 1970 elections were held for New York's representatives to the U.S. Congress, Badillo ran as a candidate from New York's Twenty-First Congressional District —a district that includes El Barrio, or East Harlem. Not surprisingly, Badillo won an easy victory in the election.

Herman Badillo

As the sole Puerto Rican in the U.S. Congress, Herman Badillo has become the most influential political leader of the Puerto Rican community in this country. A member of the Education and Labor Committee, Badillo has worked for the betterment of *all* disadvantaged Americans—not just Puerto Ricans. Although Congressman Badillo seems assured of being reelected to the U.S. House of Representatives, he still has hopes of one day becoming the mayor of New York City.

2. *Business*

With the help of the Puerto Rican Merchants Association, the Small Business Administration, and other organizations, thousands of Puerto Ricans have established businesses of their own on the mainland. Although most of these businesses are small, their owners take great pride in them. And this pride is understandable, for the many Puerto Rican restaurants, grocery stores, and garment shops established in this country have added a real Latin flavor to such mainland cities as New York, Chicago, and Boston.

While most of the Puerto Rican businessmen in this country have been content with their small businesses, a few Puerto Ricans have built their businesses up into flourishing enterprises. Manuel A. Casiano, Jr., Julio Hernández, and Nick Lugo are three of the most ambitious and successful Puerto Rican businessmen on the mainland. Each has established a thriving business, and each had helped the Puerto Rican community in this country.

Manuel A. Casiano, Jr., is an ex-delivery boy who became a self-made millionaire by establishing his own motion picture business in this country. After selling his lucrative business, he went on to become the national director of Puerto Rico's migration office in New York. Then, he was appointed as the administrator of the Economic Development Program in Puerto Rico. Casiano has been an important leader of New York's Puerto Rican community, and he has been involved in numerous Puerto

Manuel A. Casiano

Rican organizations over the years. When asked about the future of the Puerto Ricans on the mainland, he said, "Give us 20 years, and you'll say: 'They made it—just like the Jews and Italians and everybody else who came here, struggled and won.'"

One of the founders of the Puerto Rican Merchants Association, Julio Hernández grew up in New York City during the Great Depression. Since there were 10 people in his family, Julio knew poverty and hunger as a child. Yet, he and his seven brothers and sisters all managed to finish high school. After marrying and settling down in Brooklyn, Hernández opened a grocery store and a restaurant. These businesses were so successful that Hernández soon expanded them into larger enterprises. Encouraged by his own success as a businessman, he helped organize the Puerto Rican Merchants Association—an organization dedicated to promoting small businesses among the Puerto Ricans in New York. In addition to playing a leading role in this organization, Hernández has been involved in many Puerto Rican civic organizations, community centers, and charitable organizations.

Nick Lugo is another Puerto Rican businessman who became a self-made millionaire on the mainland. Born in Puerto Rico,

Nick Lugo

he and his family moved to New York City in 1930. By washing dishes and folding shirts, Nick Lugo saved up enough money to open a real estate and travel office in 1940. Today, this shrewd businessman is the owner and head executive of the Cophresi Travel Agency, which has over 30 branches on the U.S. mainland and in Puerto Rico. Like Manuel Casiano and Julio Hernández, Nick Lugo is involved in many civic organizations and is an active leader of New York's Puerto Rican community.

3. *Literature and the Arts*

In 1955, Governor Muñoz Marín initiated an important cultural program in Puerto Rico called "Operation Serenity." That same year, the Institute of Puerto Rican Culture was established on the island. Still in existence, the institute is dedicated to preserving Spanish traditions and to promoting the arts on the island. A number of cultural organizations similar to the Institute of Puerto Rican Culture have likewise been established by the Puerto Ricans living on the U.S. mainland. New York City is home to two of these organizations—the *Instituto de Puerto Rico* and the

Ateneo de Puerto Rico. Like the Institute of Puerto Rican Culture, these mainland organizations are attempting to promote literature, music, and the arts among the Puerto Ricans.

Under the guidance of the Instituto de Puerto Rico and the Ateneo de Puerto Rico, several groups of Puerto Ricans have established their own theater companies. One of these, the Puerto Rican Traveling Theatre, presents Puerto Rican dramas in the streets of New York each summer. This theater group has been a tremendous success, and it has helped familiarize the Puerto Ricans of New York with the works of such Puerto Rican playwrights as Luis Florens Torres, René Marqués, Francisco Arriví, and Emilio Belaval.

The Puerto Rican Traveling Theatre performs in the streets of El Barrio.

In the world of literature, at least two individuals of Puerto Rican ancestry have distinguished themselves as outstanding American writers. The late poet-essayist-playwright William Carlos Williams was born in New Jersey in 1883. Since his mother was a native of Puerto Rico, Williams felt a strong bond

William Carlos Williams

with the island and its people. Ironically, Williams had never intended to become a writer. In fact, he was a practicing doctor for over 40 years before he turned to writing as a profession. In his *Autobiography*, Williams explained that it was through working with the sick and afflicted that he gained insight into the "secret gardens of the self." And it was this deep, personal insight that inspired him to turn from medicine to writing.

One of Williams's first major successes was the poem *Paterson*, which he wrote between 1946 and 1958. This long, complex poem gives a fascinating and detailed history of an American city and its people. A collection of Williams's essays was published in 1954, and a collection of his plays in 1961. Two years later, Williams was awarded the Pulitzer Prize in poetry for his brilliant poem *Pictures from Breughel*. Soon after receiving the award, the talented writer died.

The contemporary writer Piri Thomas has also distinguished himself as a gifted poet and novelist. His most important work to date has been *Down These Mean Streets*, an autobiographical novel published in 1967. Highly acclaimed by the critics, the best selling book tells the story of Thomas's life in the ghettoes of East Harlem. Thomas became addicted to drugs as a young man, and much of his hard-hitting book deals with the drug subculture of El Barrio. *Down These Mean Streets* was such a success that in 1968, Harlem-born filmmaker José García turned the book into an award-winning documentary entitled *The World of Piri Thomas*. Thomas is a very talented writer, and he shows the promise of producing many more fine novels.

Piri Thomas

Several Puerto Ricans in this country have also made significant achievements in the field of classical music. A native of Puerto Rico, bass singer Justino Díaz has sung with the New England Opera Theatre, the Opera Company of Boston, the American Opera Society, and the Metropolitan Opera Company at New York's Lincoln Center.

Like Justino Díaz, concert pianist Jesús María Sanromá was born in Puerto Rico. After moving to the U.S. mainland in 1917, he studied piano at the New England Conservatory of Music. In 1926 he was appointed as the official pianist of the Boston Symphony Orchestra. Since then, Sanromá has given recitals in London, Paris, Vienna, Madrid, and scores of American cities. Each year, the pianist plays at the annual summer concert at the University of Puerto Rico.

Justino Díaz

Jesús María Sanromá

Born in Spain, the world-famous cellist and conductor Pablo Casals came to Puerto Rico in 1956 to visit the birthplace of his mother. Casals liked the island so much that he decided to settle there. In 1957 he founded the annual Casals Music Festival in Puerto Rico. Later, the outstanding musician helped establish the Puerto Rico Symphony Orchestra. Although Casals has taken up residence in France and the U.S. mainland, he returns to Puerto Rico almost every year to play for the island and the people he loves.

Pablo Casals

4. *Sports*

Many Puerto Rican athletes have won fame and fortune in this country through their outstanding achievements in sports. In fact, the Puerto Ricans can boast of heroes in such diverse athletic fields as baseball, boxing, horse racing, golf, and tennis.

A number of Puerto Ricans have made names for themselves as major league baseball players. During World War II, Hiram Bithorn pitched for the Chicago White Sox while Luis Olmo served as an outfielder for the Brooklyn Dodgers. Later, during the 1950s, Rubén Gómez and Luis "Tite" Arroya pitched for several different National League and American League teams.

Hiram Bithorn   **Luis Olmo**

Today, Roberto Clemente and Orlando Cepeda are two of the most outstanding baseball players in the States. Roberto Clemente was born in Carolina, Puerto Rico, in 1934. After playing professional baseball in Puerto Rico, Clemente came to the U.S. mainland in 1955 and joined the Pittsburg Pirates as an outfielder. A perennial Golden Glove winner, a four-time National League batting champion, and the Most Valuable Player of the

Rubén Gómez

Year in 1966, Clemente is considered a phenomenon by many baseball fans and sports writers. In 1971 he was named the Most Valuable Player of the World Series. Many fans believe that if it had not been for Clemente's spectacular catching and batting, the Pittsburg Pirates would not have won the World Series against the Baltimore Orioles that year.

Like Clemente, island-born Orlando Cepeda is a first-rate baseball player. After moving to the States in 1958, Cepeda joined the San Francisco Giants as a first baseman. Eight years

Roberto Clemente

Orlando Cepeda

later he joined the St. Louis Cardinals, and in 1969, the Atlanta Braves. After playing with the Braves, Cepeda joined the Oakland Athletics. The outstanding first baseman was named Rookie Player of the Year in 1958, and the Most Valuable Player of the Year in 1967.

In the world of boxing, three Puerto Ricans have been hailed as world champions. The first was Sixto Escobar, who became the World Bantamweight Boxing Champion in 1936. He lost the title in 1937, regained it in 1938, and vacated it in 1939. Following in Escobar's footsteps was José Torres, who won the title of World Light-Heavyweight Boxing Champion in 1965 by defeating Willie Pastrano of Miami, Florida. After holding the title for two years, Torres lost it in 1967 to Dick Tiger of Nigeria. During the same year that Torres lost his title, Carlos Ortiz won the title of World Lightweight Boxing Champion—for the fifth time! Then, in 1968, he lost the title to Carlos Cruz of the Dominican Republic.

Boxing and baseball are not the only sports in which the Puerto Ricans have excelled. Eddie Belmonte has won international fame as a prizewinning horse jockey; Charlíto Pasarell, as an outstanding tennis player; and Juan "Chi Chi" Rodríguez, as a top-

Sixto Escobar

José Torres

Eddie Belmonte   **Charlíto Pasarell**   **"Chi Chi" Rodríguez**

notch golfer. Of the three, Rodríguez is probably the best known. Born in Bayamón, Puerto Rico, in 1935, the former caddie became a professional golfer in 1960. Four years later, Rodríguez was one of the leading tournament and money winners of the Professional Golf Association. In 1967 he won the famed Texas Open Golf Tournament, and in 1968, the Sahara International. The following year he represented Puerto Rico in the World Cup Tournament in Singapore. Although he did not win the top prize of the tournament, he played exceptionally well and won much praise for his performance.

5. *Entertainment*

As in the world of sports, several individuals of Puerto Rican ancestry have distinguished themselves in the entertainment world. Among them are José Feliciano, Chita Rivera, Rita Moreno, and José Ferrer.

Blind since birth, singer-guitarist-composer José Feliciano was born in Larez, Puerto Rico, in 1945. Five years later he moved with his family to New York City. Feliciano taught himself how to play the guitar at the age of nine. When he was 17, he began his professional career by performing at a number of coffeehouses in New York's Greenwich Village. Then, in the summer of 1968, he won national recognition with his Latin-soul version of the song "Light My Fire." Recording contracts, nightclub engagements, television appearances, and a long string of other hits (including "Walk Right In") followed. The self-taught musician won two Grammy Awards in 1968: one, for the Best New Artist of the Year; the other, for the Most Popular Singer of the Year.

José Feliciano

Dolores Conchita del Rivero shortened her name to Chita Rivera after she became a singing-dancing-acting star of Broadway. The vibrant performer first took dancing lessons when she was 11. At the age of 14, she won a scholarship to the School of American Ballet in New York. A few years later, she landed a featured dancing role in the musical *Call Me Madam*. More major roles in *Guys and Dolls, Can-Can, Seventh Heaven, Bye Bye Birdie*, and other Broadway musicals followed. To date, her most important role has been as the fiery, flamboyant Anita in the

Broadway musical *West Side Story*. In addition to her work on Broadway, Miss Rivera has appeared on television and in movies. In 1968 she starred with Shirley MacLaine and Ricardo Montalban in *Sweet Charity*, one of the major motion picture musicals of the year.

While Chita Rivera played the role of Anita in the Broadway version of *West Side Story*, Puerto Rican actress Rita Moreno (Rosa Dolores Alverio) won fame playing the same role in the motion picture version of the musical. For her outstanding performance in the movie, she won an Academy Award as the Best Supporting Actress of 1962. Miss Moreno was born in Humacao, Puerto Rico, in 1931. When she was six, she went to New York with her mother (her parents were divorced). Two years later, the young performer began singing and dancing at a nightclub in Greenwich Village. At 17, Miss Moreno starred in her first Broadway play, and at 18 she signed a contract with Metro-Goldwyn-Mayer. Prior to *West Side Story*, she appeared in such films as *Singin' in the Rain*, *Seven Cities of Gold*, and *The King and I*. Since *West Side Story*, she has starred in *Popi*, *Carnal Knowledge*, and several other films.

Rita Moreno in a lively scene from *West Side Story*

José Ferrer

Another Puerto Rican Academy Award winner is José Ferrer. Born in Santurce, Puerto Rico, in 1912, the talented actor won the 1950 Oscar for Best Actor of the Year for his moving performance in *Cyrano de Bergerac*. After this success, Ferrer went on to star in such notable films as *Moulin Rouge*, *The Caine Mutiny*, *Lawrence of Arabia*, *Ship of Fools*, and *Enter Laughing*. Then, in 1966, he starred in the smash Broadway hit *The Man of La Mancha*.

Conclusion

In a very real sense, the story of the Puerto Ricans on the U.S. mainland has only just begun. Even the first Puerto Ricans to migrate to this country came here less than 100 years ago. But one thing is certain: nearly 2 million Puerto Ricans are living on the mainland, and they are here to stay. As their story unfolds, the Puerto Ricans will continue to make a unique contribution to this country—a country made up of many different peoples working together for the good of all.

The IN AMERICA *Series*

We specialize in publishing quality books for
young people. For a complete list please write:

LERNER PUBLICATIONS COMPANY
241 First Avenue North, Minneapolis, Minnesota 55401